O' THE HAPPY PINES

BY DUNCAN T. CULLMAN

DORRANCE
PUBLISHING CO
EST. 1920
PITTSBURGH, PENNSYLVANIA 15238

Dorrance Publishing Co
585 Alpha Drive
Suite 103
Pittsburgh, PA 15238
Visit our website at *www.dorrancebookstore.com*

ISBN: 978-1-6461-0180-1
eISBN: 978-1-6461-0540-3

I dedicate this book to my father as a reminder of valuing education. To my dogs and cat for their kindheartedness. Also, my family and skier friends.

The beauty and acknowledgment of the happy pines, we say thank you. thank you for all the trees, flowers, and plants, as well as birds and nature.

O' THE HAPPY PINES

MY FRIEND IS A DOG NAMED RUSIO

My friend is a dog named Rusio

He lives in a country called Chile

Which is shaped roughly like a strand of spaghetti

In the north it is very dry and is a desert

In the south of Chile it rains a lot where Rusio lives, in Villarica.

Sometimes in winter it snows in Chile but usually in the high Andes Mountains

But sometimes it snows down low in the towns.

No one knows where Rusio came from, only Rusio

Just a year ago today he arrived in town. Probably he was abandoned by an irresponsible, bad owner.

He was discovered first by one nearly dawn tourist, who noticed the hungry dog and went to the nearby market to buy him some dog food and snacks.

The tourist went to sleep very sad that night because he was worrying about his new friend, the dog named Rusio.

"Rusio" was a named picked for the dog by various local shopkeepers because he was a blond short-haired dog, so they gave him a name that means "Russian."

Rusio seemed to have a friend who was another dog named Oranginho, who was colored like an orange (and probably a Chinese Chow dog). Oranginho followed Rusio everywhere they ran, side by side. Oranginho wanted to know where Rusio was getting his food.

Someone had been feeding Rusio steak and roast beef. Was it the lady Madelyn in Artes Sur who sold wool hats and socks? Or was it the lady Michelle who sold wooden bowls? She came here from France for love and married, but her husband passed away. Or was it Giovanni, the cook at Balganez Restaurant, where business was slow in winter season? Or was it that same tourist who are kuchen tortas at Kuchenladen with his afternoon tea?

A cloud of sweet-smelling gas followed Rusio wherever he went. That was why Oranginho followed him everywhere. He wanted to be so popular like Rusio, who seemingly had friends everywhere all over the town but growled now at Oranginho to please stand out of his way and not smother him.

Who, for instance, had bought Rusio the new pea green leather collar with dangling miniature milk bones?

Everyone loved Rusio even though he had no home but just wandered around the entire town.

Let's see if we can find Rusio a nice home somewhere where he can be warm and not starving, where no cars will run him over in the street!

He is my friend, Rusio, and he is a dog! Bring him home, someone, please! And bring me home, too. I am a homeless person named Agostino. We all need to be loved and find a home to shield us from the storms!

EDUCATION
EDUCATION IS A PERSONAL CHOICE

How good it is to have a friend!

Now we know twice as much as I myself alone

And especially an older friend who is wise,

Seasoned by many years yet well,

Healthy as though saved by some morality.

Good habits are like a strong back brace,

Those who continue to survive have learned the natural laws,

Our common code of behavior when dealing with others...

We cling to righteousness and to those who are just,

Our friends treat us with respect and dignity.

Our bodies are our temples and our minds

Are mostly filled with fond memories

Of dear friends, some no longer living

But living in us in our dearest chapel,

The human mind, a friend and steward of our planet.

My best friend, my mind, I treat it with respect and remain sober and alert

To the winds of change, to our new surroundings.

We move forward in time but look both ways

Back at memories of friends but forward

To new friends who rise on our horizon

Like the sun itself, like planets in space, like new dancers on the grandest stage!

(School is now any environment where you find friends, the center of which who bears responsibility for the safety of all is our teacher, Rabbi.)

BEARS VISIT SANTIAGO,
A CHILDREN'S BOOK

"What are bears doing in Santiago?"

Bears eat berries.

Bears love honey.

When it's cold, bears hibernate.

Then they wake up hungry!

"What's all that noise?" ask the curious bears.

"There's a city down there in all that smog and noise!"

"Many garbage cans surrounded by barking dogs!"

The dogs stop barking when the warm sun rises to warm the sidewalk.

"Now that the dogs are asleep, we can go to Santiago," say the bears.

"We don't have wallets, so nobody can rob us in the subway."

"We don't have backpacks, so nobody can pick through them while we walk."

"We don't have passports, so they won't think we're rich gringo tourists."

"What do we need taxis for?" proclaim the bears.

"We are bears! We go where we want to!"

The policeman lets us cross the street.

The cars stop and people stare at us.

The signs all say,

"Don't feed the bears!"

The grocery man throws oranges at us and runs away.

"We want the blueberries and look, some peanuts!"

"Bears eat anything at all and everything," say the passing schoolchildren!

"Run," says their teacher, "run, children, run!"

"We 're not scared of bears," say the children.

(Fear is something they accidentally taught us in school.)

"We're not afraid either!" say the hungry bears.

"Look, the supermarket shelves are empty."

Bears don't even carry credit cards.

Dogs have woken up now from all this commotion.

Dogs are barking wildly in the street.

"Let's go home," say the bears.

"Follow that bus that says 'San Jose de Maipo,'" says Papa Bear.

"Yes, that's the bus," says Mama Bear.

The bus driver sees the bears, stops the bus, and runs to the subway.

"Board the bus, all my cubbies!" says Papa Bear.

"Mama Bear didn't lose her license; she can drive!"

All the bears go home to Cajon de Maipo, where they climb,

Where they climb some more, up and up,

Into the mighty Andes Mountains.

"There are no bears in Chile!" says a policeman! (He doesn't understand climate change.)

"We know better. We are the bears!"

O' THE HAPPY PINES

Whenever I shall return to New Hampshire

There the happy pine trees with arms unfolded

Outstretched long, brazen branches like arms

That reach upward as though to embrace the sun

And heaven itself in some kind of a laughter or great joy

How they greet me, so many happy pines

Not that the spruces or firs are any less happy, nor any less green

But the deciduous trees in winter have all fallen asleep

Saving their joy for perhaps May until September

So more it's these happiest of pines I see in winter months, too

With arms unfurled, grasping at heaven in warm embrace

Even though the sun may have just set or still may rise.

What friends I have whose smiles are like unfurled arms of pines

Whose laughter inspires even the gods

Who are perhaps only are no more than the cherubim and seraphim

Perhaps their arms are like these pine branches curled upward

Unfurled downward from heaven somewhere

For I have miles to drive before I sleep

And my companion is so asleep inside my oversized down parka

Somewhere she has gone near the lakes edge on a July afternoon

Beneath so many tall pines in northern New England, perhaps

Or perhaps she is in Colorado or New Mexico or Arizona?

These pine trees seem to be everywhere that trees exist

So they must be in Heaven too with my friends who have passed

Now the white eerie moon arises to illuminate my cruel world

Many of my pets have passed likewise and died cruel deaths

Likewise my time remaining here has grown shorter than I can even imagine

So I must unfurl my arms and reach upward in warm embrace

I hope there is a reason for all this love that trees express in gentle breezes

I hope there is a loving God that made these trees to grow and sing their song

So I must try to sing and hope like the happy pines

I must try to embrace just as my own mother held out her arms

To hold me close to her breasts, that I may nurture and thrive

Like O' these happy pines....

A LOGGER'S REMORSE

Menorah-shaped bushy treetops of

These lovely pines in their silent constant prayer

How could anyone of right mind

Cut down a living tree?

Far worse than kidnapping or blasphemy

Is the logger's quota in board feet

And the mill itself with jagged saw teeth is a hungry devil possessed.

Because these pines and firs stand like sentinels

Guardians of our mother, this planet Earth

Waving their long arms at us with every passing breeze.

DUNCAN T. CULLMAN

So my entire young manhood was wasted clutching a chainsaw

As though I were achieving some great purpose

More than sheer obsessive destruction of the Earth itself.

This giant chainsaw in hand, I the mighty tyrant

Whose marriage was soon doomed by God Himself intervening.

And now the birches themselves sprouting buds...

It is mid-spring and these woodlands

All shout with joy and benediction and praise…

APOLOGIES TO TREES

All my heartfelt apologies to so many trees

Through bicycling many miles over hill and vale

I felt your keen presence on every horizon

You stood like centurions, unmovable and still

In your predestined locations and I in mine

Should I feel sorry for us, no

What a waste of time that would be to droop

Like some willow on a hot summer day, though rare

So we all stand tall and proud and breathe in the air or exhale it

From photosynthesis or vitamin D, whichever

Because I need you high on the ski mountain, I am lonely and long for your protection and shelter below tree line

I have never really been alone except in some windowless jail cell

I have always had you trees for friends because you are

The greatest of friends never disappointing me

Causing me to breathe, I fill my lungs with your great gift of air

At night you give me carbon dioxide but I am asleep, requiring no great energy

But at sunrise you feed me the oxygen I require

So naturally I should hold you in reverence and offer my great thanks

Until when I shall be no more but my remains shall be just molecules and atoms, and you shall need these

I may then serve you more perfectly then and my remains may then become trees.

Such noble creatures, so obedient to their creator, unlike most of mankind

So that I must apologize for humankind and the insensitivity of loggers and timber companies,

The greedy corporations who go about each day destroying our mother planet for the sake of only profit

Whose financial donations to equally greedy politicians who likewise destroy our planet

While trees grow up in perfect radiance and fill our horizons with such joy

Their branches shade us on a hot day as though in great pity

Because they are so loving these trees while we are not, though we pretend to be every church service

When Christ had been raised upon His cross on some horizon, He beheld some trees who took pity

The Roman soldiers were not supposed to show such emotion, but trees always do

Pity us all then because we are so distant to our God, but the trees bring us all so much closer because they all are....

THE LONELY PINE

The lonely, sad pine tree

Whose branches drooped down, perhaps from weight of wet snow clumps

Had so many brother and sister pines all so happy

With arms up, stretched to heaven

As if to grasp the sun itself in warm embrace

But more so in deep appreciation of their creator

The everlasting God, our father

Now that winter is over, when leafy trees are budding

How they now all yawn after a long winter's sleep, so leafless and bare

Shall I rise up too like all these obedient trees

Shall I no longer stoop my weary back

From winter's long chores and life's long pain and suffering

To give glory to my God and break forth in song

Like the green meadow, like the warming cows, now happier

Will I be happier too or is it just of a short season, my joy?

I had been a rambunctious youth and suffered calamities from my follies

So that now I am more cautious and reverent

And my respect for all these beauteous trees is improved

I cherish them too, not just my kin and pets

For this earth is like a mother to me now that mine has long departed

She was benevolent in her own style and way

She had class and knew such secrets as the earth would subtly reveal to her

She had been stout like these tall pines but then weathered with time and clumps of heavy snow

Just as I too now saddened to remember her struggles

This life on earth not easy at all, and so we struggle onward to our too-early graves

I now know there is a God because these trees have revealed to me their hidden joy

I know there is a joy in me that swells when I see trees in the very distance and some are pines....

APOLOGIES TO PEOPLE

My sincere apologies to everyone (including all you people),

Friends and relatives, foes and adversaries, enemies, et cetera

We are less than Divine without Christ or some equivalent

In other words, we are less than the angels, perhaps dim shadows of them at best,

We are fallen angels because of the liberties of our selfishness

Which backfire upon us daily. We make plans that come to naught,

We have some dreams that are only dreams

We had mostly hoped for some great accomplishments

Most of which turned into dour disappointments

But still we hope to at least be friends, if possible

As there is little else to bond us together beyond our common misery.

Well spoken. You might add your fitting verses to this essay.

So I write of mostly people who were mostly older than me who have come and gone

I cannot write of you who are not yet born but only wish you well.

I write for readers who may toss my words onto some forgotten shelf in the library of a decaying house

I write to unborn readers to wish them luck, that they may somehow change this equation of human suffering

I write from my heart to yours, that you might rise up and fly like eagles on high

To soar over the mountaintops and see the rising sun beyond the breaking waves

I write of centuries now past and of all our brief recorded history,

Tyrants have come and gone. It is the nature of the beast….

This earth is not heaven, we realize that much.

Hopefully we shall all rise from these ashes and be angels once again

To sing our songs of praise like choir children in their great achievement

We all sing Hallelujahs and Amen forevermore....

THE TREES

The bushy top of almost every pine tree

Is a Menorah and testimony that God loves us all

All these trees do testify to this

Though they have no eyes to see

Their branches are like fingers of a hand reaching upward

In meditation and prayer, which is all each knows

So where have I been most of my life, I had not realized this

I was like a blind and ignorant man with no heart at all.

Surely I noticed every passing female of young beauty,

But now I notice just as much these trees

Who are so reverent to their Creator

And just today there were so many loving spruces and firs

Who now accept me also into their joyous throng

How they sing too this joyful music, so sweet to my ears

I had been so hardened and set fast in my youthful ignorance

Not to notice all of God's children, but now I have a new life

I am like a deciduous tree which has slept through a long, lonely winter

And now the warm air blows over the earth with plentiful sunshine, spring is here

So let me bloom and burst forth from bud my many splendored green leaves to make oxygen and breath

Let me breathe all of this, let me stand tall and feel the wind upon my branches

Let my heart be free to skip and dance and love

Let my youthful glee be contagious to all who see me in their midst

Let me be among friends and laugh and sing of all that is heartfelt and true

And let God be present in my land wherever I go so that peace prevails and justice

So all my brethren be free as well and that we are now of God's great liberation

So rejoice for summer nears in this, our garden Paradise!

DUNCAN T. CULLMAN

DUNCAN T. CULLMAN

DUNCAN T. CULLMAN

DUNCAN T. CULLMAN

DUNCAN T. CULLMAN

DUNCAN T. CULLMAN

BLACK FOREST

My father and I travelled to Germany because he had taken a new job, but he could not discuss it with me. We had to go there, but it just so happened he brought his new lady friend along. Her name was Kip and she had an eight-year-old son named Wallace, who was big for his age and quite tough, indeed.

My mother was out of the picture now, as she had decided to rebel and be a witch with many witchlike friends and sorcerers. Her family was from Salem and Cohasset, Massachusetts, where they do that sort of thing. Anyway, an ambulance came and took her away one day after lunch.

So Wallace and I fought continually, first in Germany, then in France, where camels and Arabs paraded daily on the sidewalk in Paris. But then we drove through the Ardennes Forest on our way to the Black Forest on our way to Switzerland, Italy, and Marseille, France again, then Mallorca, Spain.

There were many trials for walking into the Black Forest in Germany, but it was very dark and wonderful but almost scary to those from southern climates like New York, where there is much more sun in big, broad, deciduous leaves.

The Black Forest is tall, dark spruce trees and pine and fir, the trees being so tall that only single spills of light hit the forest floor somewhere distant through the trees but not on the trail itself.

I became quite sick with some kind of a fever.

My father instructed me to just sit on the available bench where we stopped, that they would continue but return this way again. I agreed and lay down on the bench and must have fallen asleep, although I did not realize it.

Suddenly a man appeared quite close to me, sitting on another bench, and he was very old, with white hair and a long white beard. He even called me by my name, and I listened to him because he knew everything. He knew my past and he knew my future as well.

"Tobias, you will have to decide in your life whether you are a Jew or not a Jew." He knew I had been adopted and suggested that I would have the liberty to decide for myself exactly what I might want to become, implying that it was up to me to be of good conscience and decide exactly what might be required in my circumstances, which would develop with complexity.

I was puzzled by his assessment and turned to ask him a question, but he disappeared and the bench he sat on disappeared with him.

My father shook me and I finally woke up, saying,

"There was a man here."

"I don't see anyone," said my father, "you've had a dream, that's all."

WHAT PEANUT BUTTER DID
TO MY MORTAL HUMAN BODY

"Peanut butter is delicious," said my father.

I was a very picky eater as a child, plus we were going to a tropical country, where the salads were full of microbes.

Thus we bought peanut butter canisters weighing five pounds each.

I was more than four years old when I began eating mostly peanut butter and a highly vegetarian diet. I loved olive oil and sunflower oil and all things from the plant world. My father was a travelling salesman and took me all over the world with him, as my mother had died and a governess would be more expensive in the United States than in third-world countries like Colombia, where breakfast consisted of every imaginable fruit on our planet.

There were fish in the ocean and my father tried in vain to persuade me to eat something other than peanut butter, but since the fish in the tropical markets all had eyes I felt very guilty eating them or guinea pigs still alive in burlap sacks in Peru. How could anyone eat them or even choose to eat any living animal?

I preferred pineapples and even decaffeinated coffee with mostly boiled hot milk.

In Paraguay I drank too much yerba mate before my father realized it was full of caffeine, which made my heart race and his, too. We raced around everywhere, even to Tierra del Fuego, the land of penguins. I could not imagine eating them, although I was told that Mapuche or Araucanian Indians boiled them in stew.

I preferred my peanut butter and grew up on it until even my college days at the University of Cameroon, which is in Africa, the land of peanuts and lima beans. I preferred those too and even anything with large quantities of vegetable oil.

I fell in love with my opposite, a young woman who preferred mostly eating porkchops, lambchops, and beef briskets. Our marriage didn't last very long. However, our children were quite well balanced, consuming everything in sight except the refrigerator itself.

The years flew by and I ate mostly peanut butter still, to the dismay of my now grown-up children, who thought my continuance of the peanut diet might be altering my body chemistry. Perhaps they were correct, as I was soon diagnosed with a brain disorder of some indistinguishable type. My psychiatrist gave me a brain scan and told me quite confidentially, "We don't see this kind of phenomenon in human beings very often. You are quite peculiar in that your brainwaves are more similar to plants, specifically evergreen trees and evergreen shrubs. Do you celebrate Christmas at home the entire year?"

"I am no Santa Claus!" I protested, feeling quite insulted by all of this. "But I do take long walks in the forest behind my house. There are many pine trees and spruces, balsam fir, and a few cedar trees and shrubs. It is very damp and beautiful, and yes, I do consider the trees to be my friends. I even speak to them, but they do not reply in any human words. I am no schizophrenic hearing voices, if that's what you imply. The trees have their own language, which is more like ESP or telepathy. They feel love for each other and even for me, but they do not for any lumberjack out there to murder them or their cousin trees."

I soon gave up on that psychiatrist and took even longer walks in my forest to the further dismay of my close friends and associates except for one good fellow, a biologist, but he died shortly thereafter.

Palm trees and deciduous trees never were close to me and I'm not sure why. I do eat peanuts still on all my daily and increasingly nocturnal adventures. I walk barefoot nowadays as well, not certain exactly when this began but I am enjoying the wet topsoil sinking my toes deeper and deeper.

I think I shall never return to the human rat race and its preoccupation with destroying our planet via industrialization. I am most comfortable here in my forest among trees who have proven to be my best and most long-lasting friends on this earth, especially the evergreens but now increasingly every tree and every bush and every plant.

I wiggle my toes deeply into the earth, but now they will not move, just stretch deeper and deeper, so I raise my arms higher and higher up into the stars, moon, and sun....

EIGHT YEARS OLD AND THE ARK

I was still a child and eight years old when my father and I were invited by my uncles and cousins to go to a Hebrew Synagogue on the Upper West Side of New York, not too far north of Central Park but northerly enough to be influenced by Harlem, which had become an African-American neighborhood. We took a taxi there. I remember it as being early autumn.

I considered myself a baseball player at the time with a bright future in Little League. We had great coaches with moral values. I played for the Catholic team the Knights of Columbus, but in a few years I would change to the Kiwanis team, sponsored by the Masons, I cannot remember exactly, as I was more interested in the game of baseball, Mickey Mantle, Yogi Berra, and Roger Maris of the New York Yankees.

So we all crowded into this apartment and over by the piano, well, it looked like a piano but it was golden, a big, mysterious-looking thing. I have never seen anything like that ever since or before.

"Don't look at it," my father warned me.

So we went to our seats and someone turned out the lights. And my cousins, who were devoted Hebrews, warned me not to open my eyes because God was going to come out of that contraption and would kill us if we dared to open our eyes.

And someone said that maybe it wasn't working at all.

And someone else said to be quiet, God was just not yet sure about us, that we had to be more sincere.

We waited. If God was coming out of that box, there was no way I was going to miss the show and suddenly as I opened my eyes a light came crawling out of the box and saw my open eyes, uh-oh.

I passed out cold.

There were creatures of all shapes and sizes, of all creations, in all planets, all seraphim, and I was totally afraid like never in my entire life, and then came some cherubim and perhaps some angels.

I lay on the floor when the lights came back on in the room but I was still unconscious there, surrounded by my unbelieving cousins, including Susan, who said something to the effect that I must have opened my eyes and was indeed dead.

Suddenly I woke up from my spell and I had not seen God but had seen too much and had been terribly afraid, but now I was overjoyed to see my cousins laughing at me.

GINA,
MY LOVE,

In the morning you are here to great my new day

Like the sun warming my every shivering appendage

Like a kiss to connect me to the memory of my mother

Who first brought me into this world

To know of your love.

Father, I learned to love you too from your love

You were there to keep all our love from spoiling into passion and temper

You were like the cold blue sky

Ever constant, ever deep like eternity

This eternal love because our mother earth keeps on spinning

'Round and 'round like your arms wrapped all around me and your legs

To support the foundation of us, we are family

Even dogs and cats with our many babies

Fish and flying things, birds singing in the trees, now sprouting

Light green budding like our love.

When I first saw your face

We were both married to other unfaithfuls,

Never imagining that one day we might yet discover in each other

True and lasting love, it is like a songbird singing

Or like a soft warm breeze,

And so I kissed you or

No, you kissed me.

How did this happen?

From out of nowhere our grand collision in space,

We were just meant to be

In love

Atop whitest mountain peaks, skiing, snowboarding, and snowshoeing

Singing our song and dancing our dance

Of life and love

For they are one and we

Are the inheritors of the Truth.

DUNCAN T. CULLMAN

OUR LOVE

In this morbid world there is disease, pestilence, and plague

But under the canopy of your love

I am now among the anointed

As though my covenant with you

Is given by God and is a covenant with the Lord most high.

Many waves pound upon our shore,

There are those who do not believe God is good,

And do not receive love, just hate instead

They are bitter toward us and jealous

Because we are a mighty Citadel,

A mountaintop castle among the clouds

Majestic and high with waterfalls

That fall from Zion. Our love

Is like a limitless fountain

It gushes forth abundantly from hidden springs

To bring us joy this Holiday season

And shines like a beacon of hope, a lighthouse

For many still lost upon the sea of despair

HOMEWORK TONIGHT
AND THE LESSON IS TO LOOK AND SEE!

For everything be most glad

Because God is constantly at work

Bringing us to His Salvation

Through every little thing is our grace to be perfected

Everything is by His Gratitude toward us, whereby we might see Him

As He actually is because we actually will behold His magnificence

From the New Jerusalem, which is perfect as is a diamond

There in the Garden of Eden, guarded by the cherubim

Now we see in a blurred vision, but soon we will behold what we sincerely believe to be true

Is indeed true, that we are not alone and never were.

Our Creator has created us in His very image

For if not how might we imagine Him? He is no alien.

It is Satan, that he alienated us from our true compassionate selves

To form us into an image of selfishness and greed, lust and debauchery.

Rise up from death now, mortal man, for your day shall come with no sunset

When your doubt and despair shall be overcome

Then you will need your earthly body no more but shall obtain a new heavenly body

You shall be mine alone in paradise and forevermore.

So be enthusiastic about this final truth, which will prevail

We will all be together again with seraphim and cherubim

Where night cannot go because the illumination of our God

Is everlasting and permeates all existence

So have faith that what I say is true, that God cares

And shall deliver us to this great victory to be with Him

Where He shall wipe away every tear and replace all sadness and doubt

With hope and a great enthusiasm called praise and thankfulness.

We who are unappreciative cannot endure any hardship, and so we wither like the grass

Because there is no sustenance in us if we do not believe

This is our lesson and homework here because we are students

Most eager to understand the very meaning of our earthly lessons.

So I grab my pen and make some notes that I might remember

Lest I ever forget my enthusiasm for the truth that I might behold

From this blurred and obscure existence here in a world of misunderstanding and confusion,

Everyone is fighting and afraid, which is most exhausting,

So we require sleep and dream of what went so horribly wrong

Yet this brings us back to our lessons learned.

So the very next day we rise up, refreshed of good conscience

Or not rise at all and sink into despair and death if hope is lost.

We hope our teacher, RABBI, is present here among us

For without our shepherd we are lost sheep and leave the fold

To face utter destruction and run off some cliff chased by a bear.

I invite you to study and learn, open up a good book and read

What God has spoken is all your homework tonight

If it is home that you long for, then come

Or else be lost at sea where the great serpent shall devour your ship.

Do not let yourself be sunk but see the great lighthouse

Which beckons you home to those that love you.

WHEN THE LIGHT CAME OUT OF THAT BOX

It was darker than midnight and everyone in the room

Fell silent waiting, so perhaps half an hour passed by.

We kids thought perhaps this was a hoax

Then there was a noise inside that box

We had been forewarned not to look and not to speak

Then a light appeared, as my eyes were not one hundred percent shut.

Curiosity killed many a cat, I had been given a stern warning

Now my punishment was upon me

Many living creatures descended into my universe from some other.

There were Cherubs who were not friendly at all

While the innumerous eyes of the Lord of Hosts, who knows everything,

Were everywhere. There was a horrifying noise

As the wings of the living creature flapped to cover my eyes

If there was a hedge there or a tree, it was full of every kind of bird and a zillion eyes

The tree had no top and no bottom

Perhaps there was a river of spirits, which contained all the dead who are sleeping

As for the Tree of knowledge, it is the Tablets themselves inscrolled

In the walls of the New Jerusalem, which is white and shining

Not even the sun is so bright as heaven

And the music there if you were to hear it

Surpasses by far anything on this earth

So it would be very painful indeed to fall from such a Garden.

There is no apple there, as it must have been eaten entirely

Though there is fruit of every kind, all lit in colors more radiant than here below

Time itself does not exist there and there is no clock in Eternity

Where the Living God makes His Throne

A man cannot possibly comprehend the mind of This, Our God

So we try to comprehend the Law written for our protection

On the Wall that is the Tree of Knowledge, which is perhaps on the other side of that spiritual river from the Tree of Life, which is Love Itself

I do not know, as I was barred from entry

My passport was not stamped. I was turned around at the very Gate

And woke up finally upon the floor in a room with all its electric lights turned on, my young cousins laughing hysterically

They thought perhaps that I had died.

I had indeed seen much too much and would never quite be the same,

So neither shall you because you believe.

Come home, come back to the one who loves you

Now we fully realize that the money machine has destroyed our country

For the sake of profit, our planet earth is a ruined wasteland

The oceans are full of plastic and fracking for oil destroys groundwater

And triggers earthquakes, which cause tsunamis

While greenhouse gases do cause global warming and hurricanes

Even tornados in places where they have never seen them before

So then realize as well that big pharmaceutical companies

Have sold us increasing quantities of pills for our increasing madness

So repent of all of this. Because the kingdom of heaven is at hand!

You may not need that new sports car or customized detailed pickup

You may not need to work overtime to pay for that second home in the mountains and third home at the beach

Because your home is with a God who loves you

Who created the earth to sustain you with its beneficial climate

So why do you insist on these errant ways fed to you on television

In advertising on your Facebook page and in every magazine

Because you are sicker with every day you grow weak from sin.

It is the most serious sin of all to love any material thing at all

You love your Dunkin' Donuts coffee but you should love each other instead!

You love your morning paper in front of the television and your cigarette

You are a self-destructive naughty child that has now hit male menopause

You feel old and diabetic before your time because you are dying

And your world is dying all around you, the neighbors have bought AK47s

Has the world gone mad? Repent! Repent while you still can and

Reclaim your own life, yes, walk among the living and seek love first, not money!

Because you were created by love to be in love and to be loved, not to be this Frankenstein monster

Repent and be saved from this demon inside your iPhone inside your TV

Inside of you there is a plague called death and destruction because all because

You have grown distant from the God who loves you, who breathed life into you

That you might breathe freely and love freely this love that is the force of all the living

So why did you block the sunshine given freely that enlightened your day?

Why did you decide to hide in darkness and deceit and believe every little lie and now bigger ones

Just to earn more money, perhaps, yes, you did it to increase your salary

So you can go to Walmart and buy still a larger 3D TV screen, a five-by-ten-foot to watch the president

Because you swear he is telling you the truth as awful as it seems. Repent!

THANKFULLY PRAISE GOD
IN ALL YOUR CIRCUMSTANCES.

Bitching and complaining,

especially in a bad temperament,

is not at all a solution and may even invite sickness into your body!

No matter how severe your fate or how empty your plate,

quivering that this was all done to you, when everything actually is for the glory of God

Whereby you may learn to give thanks and glory

To the One who has allowed this big mess

In order to bring you to Salvation that you will fully understand, perfectly in God's timing

How God truly loves you, if you would open an ear

Let your voice be full of song, full of hymns

Let the energy that you block be released in order that the real you be released (these blockages are negative)

Such curses in your life...you, yourself

Children of God, think that you have brought such indifference upon yourself,

by your misunderstanding, thus encouraging sheer faith

Furthermore, give glory to God and be most appealing to others in your quest in doing so,

Let your radiance shine forth, as if the sun inside you is...

Exactly when the Lord is the sun shining, even brighter than what we see as our own sun

Leaving in its wake no darkness, no night, every tear wiped away

Joy is your salvation, simply because love has found you and filled your heart

Which has always been and forever shall be

DO NOT CHOOSE THE DARKNESS BECAUSE...

For God so created you

To walk among the living in righteousness

And delivered commandments to His people

To liberate them from sin

So do not chose the darkness because deceit waits there like a trap

You are deceived by loving objects and gadgets and machines

In a great lust for the material, you stoop down and are lost

Rise up, rise up, the final day is here and you were born for this

To fly with wings like the heart flies to a perfect stranger across a crowded room

Do not tarry, do not hesitate, go to the one who loves you

It is worth more than any paycheck

No job can bring you to this place, it is of your free will

Jobs are for money to buy things but things, no thing can buy love

Flee like a young hart upon the mountain ridges

Fly to those who love you

Come away and dwell with me in the house of the Lord, our God most high

For where I am you will be also, I have gone to prepare a room for you

Because you love nothing, you love everyone instead

HIS MAJESTY
(AND/OR HER MAJESTY)

The very Throne of God, Who resides most High

Above the judges of the earth, Whose very trillion eyes

Decipher to understand every minutest detail, of every grain of sand

The stars are all His and the oceans and the Milky Way

He is the Light of the world and the lights in Heaven

Be it understood, nothing can be hid from Him

So why bother to try and conceal the Truth

It is known to Him your every intention before you think it.

The Cherubim guard the Tree that is in His Garden

From which Adam fell and was banished

From the River of Life and the living waters

Full of every living spirit, they lie between Heaven and earth

Where the River separates the dead from the living

All who live here must die to cross it and find

His and her relatives on the far bank, where they await us like cheerleaders

Like angels most high and that is what Mother is and Father is to me, and thee.

Go now in peace because you have understanding and see

Your eyes were shut in order to behold His Light

Which sprang forth from the total darkness and silence in the Room

Because He is alive, His Light shines forth from total darkness

He spoke,

Ï AM TH(J)A)T I AM

You hear Him now still because you were chosen

To lead His people from the night into the Day

Out of that box He came with Justice and Truth to open your eyes

That you might see you were called upon to prophesize and proclaim

How great He is! How Wonderful beyond our understanding

Is THIS OUR LORD OF HOSTS, HIS MAJESTY

Beyond our comprehension

Just fear the Lord, fear what you cannot comprehend

WE FOLLOW JESUS IN OUR PROCESSION

We follow Jesus in our procession

We follow Jesus with His cross

On foot, on bicycle, on skates, on horse (but not in cars alone)

Through clouds of smog and doubt

Because His Words of Faith are the Way, are the Path

We had lost our faith, we had lost our way and stumbled

Our bride had been taken from us

We were robbed by false doctrines, by false practitioners

Who took our money but could not cure us

There is only One Healer, One Doctor for our ills

He is followed by one thousand umbrellas in a tearful procession

Through raindrops of our weeping

About the destruction of our environment

Our mother, the planet

"Come back to your mother, you lost people!"

We were conquered and sent it the captivity of despair

For our sins but we now repent

Of our lust and greed, we had lost our way in darkness

But now our Nation shall be restored to us

He will place us once again on our Holy Hill, Jerusalem, in Zion

Because hope is now lifted up within us

"Go and sin no more, pollute no more, nor sit in laziness."

"But rise up and breathe and Walk as He does!"

Now the sunshine shall be returned to us

Let us be jubilant and joyous

Now that Eden is restored, Our Garden Eternal!

We had families before but now we have only Jesus, Our Savior

I have seen Him, He is Risen

He is there in Chia, we have seen him

He is there and everywhere

Now He liberates our conquered City

Now he sets us captives free

Find Him and Live forevermore!

FLYING FREE

O how we so long to be loved!

Is it not the driving force of life itself?

But to be loved is to love others, or to not love is to choose self-destruction and death.

We try to accomplish many great things, we manipulate to acquire fame, fortune, and reputation in the world.

We stand in a great spotlight upon a grand stage and sing as though in an opera,

But a solo song is the blues and we turn blue, we need to be in harmony with a chorus,

The chorus is those who love us and care for us,

Because we are now in sync with the greater human goal,

To love for love's sake!

So visit the prisoners and feed the hungry , give shelter to the homeless,

To those that are begging give them at least pennies, nickels, and dimes

And when a friend asks us for something, give them double

When one asks for a shirt, give them two.

Those who steal shall be stolen from, those who cheat only cheat themselves, only lovers are to be admired, and those who cannot are tossed into that great sea of despair, where waves crash against their boats, driving them shipwrecked unto a rocky island

So love your neighbor as you would want to be loved

Because you are soon going away in a small vessel to another universe, where they will weigh your love, not your money (because all your money you have acquired reflects only your selfishness and lack of love). It weighs down your boat so that you have lost your freedom and mobility to be happy.

You can only be faithful without money, for what it brings is temptation and rebellion, so go to the casino and gamble it away or put it in the bank, you are better off with just a little or none. So spend it on clothes and food so you will not be naked, cold, or starving. But share with those less fortunate.

Work because you love what you do, not because you love money

Have pity and compassion on all animals and feed the hungry, and have compassion for all plants because they need water and sunlight much as you do also.

And be happy...

And sing all of this as you walk and you will be followed

Because now you are following Jesus

You are marching triumphantly

Into the sanctuary of Jerusalem, the walled city

To be with God

THE BURGLAR

So the kingdom of heaven is like a thirty-year-old burglar

Who breaks into a large mansion with ninety-nine rooms

He is looking for money or gold or jewelry

He cases the entire house, room by room

But all the rooms are empty except for some bedsheets and blankets

So he gets very hungry, wandering around ninety rooms, and goes to the kitchen

Opens the refrigerator and there is a carton of milk and

A large chocolate birthday cake with thirty candles

So he sets it on the dining room table and lights the candles

Then makes a wish that he won't be caught and blows out the candles

Eats the entire cake and drinks the entire half-gallon of milk

When lo and behold there is a loud knocking on the door

So he turns off the light and crawls behind the living room sofa.

Finally he hears the key turning the latch of the front door, which is then opened

And Santa Claus enters the house with several packages, turning on all the lights

He places them all under the Christmas tree, which he plugs in, and shouts aloud,

DUNCAN T. CULLMAN

"Merry Christmas to you, distant traveler, and welcome home."

The burglar can't control his joy and rips a very loud, stinky fart!

But Santa Claus just ignores this because he forgot the ninety-eight other

Chocolate cakes and gallons of milk, so he races back to the bakery for them

Because ninety-eight more burglars are on their way

Imagining they need gold and jewelry and cash

But God knows of their needs better than they do themselves

DUNCAN T. CULLMAN